LOTS TO SPOT

BUSY TOWN

by Genie Espinosa

WINDMILL
BOOKS

Published in 2020 by Windmill Books, an imprint of Rosen Publishing
29 East 21st Street, New York, NY 10010

Illustrations: Genie Espinosa
Text: Paul Virr
Editors: Samantha Hilton and Joe Harris

Cataloging-in-Publication Data

Names: Espinosa, Genie.
Title: Busy town / Genie Espinosa.
Description: New York : Windmill Books, 2020. | Series: Lots to spot
Identifiers: ISBN 9781538391488 (pbk.)
| ISBN 9781538391501 (library bound) | ISBN 9781538391495 (6 pack)
Subjects: LCSH: Picture puzzles–Juvenile literature.
| Cities and towns–Pictorial works–Juvenile literature.
Classification: LCC GV1507.P47 E875 2020
| DDC 793.73–dc23

Manufactured in the United States of America

CPSIA Compliance Information: Batch #BS19WM:
For Further Information contact Rosen Publishing,
New York, New York at 1-800-237-9932

CONTENT

Step inside a world of awesome puzzles!

For some, you need to spot the differences between two pictures. For others, you need to find the odd one out. You'll find all the answers at the back of the book. Turn the page to get started!

ROBOT FACTORY

Whirr! Clang! Beep! Get to work and spot
10 differences at this busy robot factory.

MALFUNCTION

One of the robots has come off the production line with a small fault. Can you see which one it is?

IN THE LAB

Oops! Which of the scientist's silhouettes is not an exact match for the scientist herself?

KINDERGARTEN

Everyone's having fun at kindergarten today!
Join in and see if you can spot 10 differences.

PRETTY PETS

Spot 10 differences between these pampered pet pictures.

LAUNDRY FUN

Get those clothes clean
and spot 10 differences, too.

AUTO REPAIRS

Pass the wrench! Help to fix these cars and find 10 differences down at the repair shop.

YEE-HAW!

Which silhouette is the only one that doesn't match the rodeo rider exactly?

TRACTOR TROUBLE

See if you can help the farmer find his tractor.
It is ever so slightly different from
all the others on this page.

FIRE STATION

Emergency! Race to the rescue
and find 10 differences.

MARKET DAY

Go shopping for 10 differences
at the farmers' market.

BLOOMING LOVELY

Which bouquet contains a single unique bloom?

SKATE SHOP

Which of the skateboards is one of a kind?

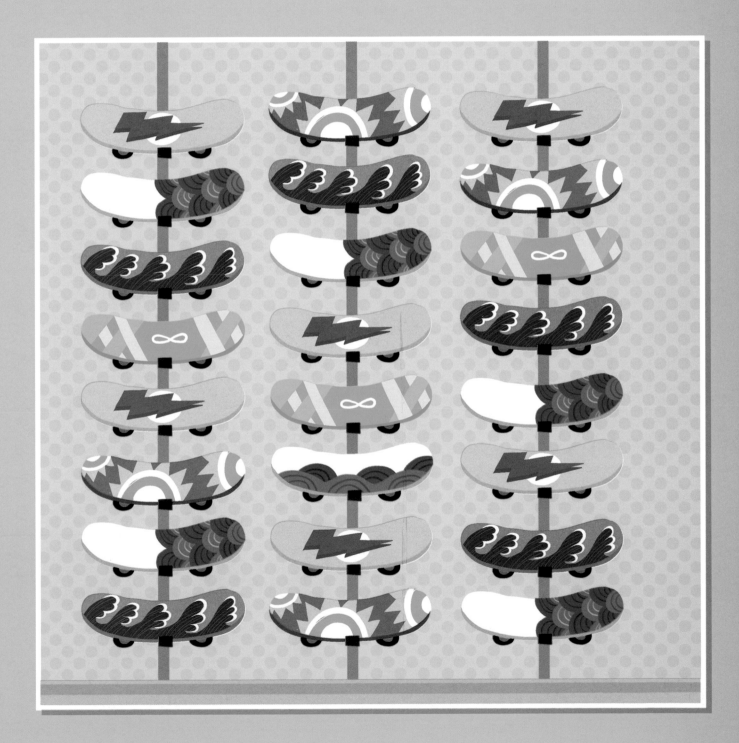

TOY STORE

Wow! Look at all these toys! Can you spot
10 differences between these toy store pictures?

LAB TEST

Which bench does not contain all of the correct equipment to perform the class experiment?

POPSICLE SPOT

Which unique treat can you spot
on the production line?

CHIC SALON

Spot 10 differences between these chic salons.

Busy Builders

Spot 10 differences between these construction sites.

PIZZA PUZZLE

First, let's find 10 differences
at this pizza restaurant.

STOP, THIEF!

The pizza thief has stolen a sneaky slice.
Which pizza has only five slices instead of six?

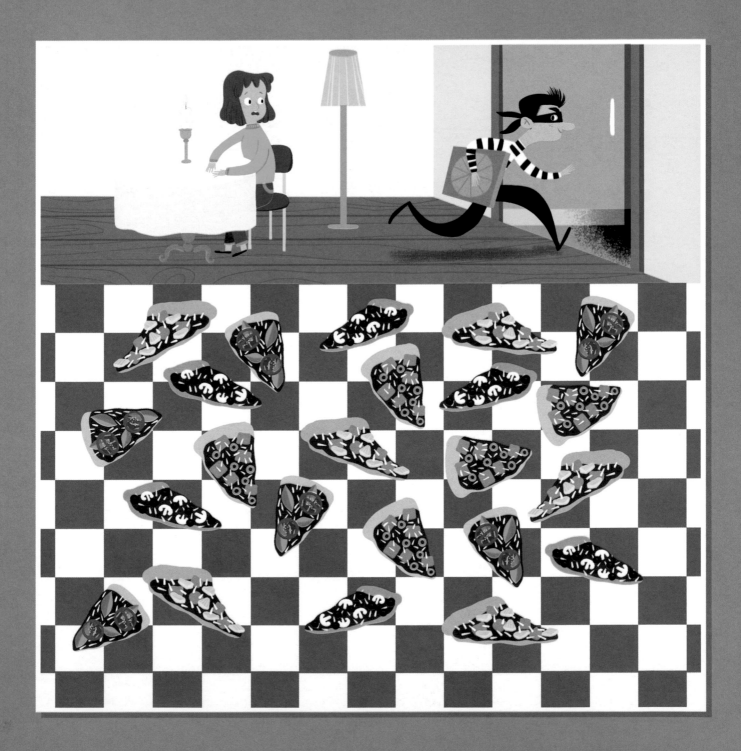

MAKING MOVIES

Spot 10 differences between these movie scenes and you could be the star of the show!

ANSWERS

Page 4-5 Robot Factory

Page 6 Malfunction

Page 7 In the Lab

Page 8-9 Kindergarten

Page 10 Pretty Pets

Page 11 Laundry Fun

Page 12-13 Auto Repairs

Page 14 Yee-Haw!

Page 15 Tractor Trouble

Page 16 Fire Station

Page 17 Market Day

Page 18 Blooming Lovely

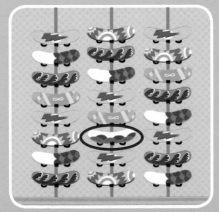

Page 19 Skate Shop

Page 20-21 Toy Store

Page 22 Lab Test

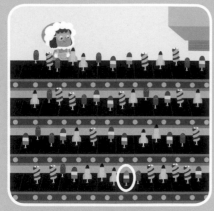

Page 23 Popsicle Spot

Page 24 Chic Salon

Page 25 Busy Builders

Page 26 Pizza Puzzle

Page 27 Stop, Thief!

Page 28-29 Making Movies